The Geeky Stitching Co's

Little Book of Cross Stitch

By Jess Payne

Published by Clink Street Publishing 2020

Copyright © 2020

First edition.

ISBN:
978-1-912262-14-4 paperback
978-1-912262-15-1 ebook

Contents

- Bloom where you are planted
- Home is where the plants are
- Celebrate the tiny victories
- Thanks a bunch
- First, I drink the coffee
- It's ok to take a break

6. Stitching for mental health & supporting charities / causes
7. FAQ's
8. Contact us

Here at the Geeky Stitching Co we are all about fun, puns & stitching up cute stuff! Operating from our rainbow coloured HQ in North Devon since 2015 we have seen tens of thousands of Cross Stitch kits head out to new homes across the globe. We are a super small husband & wife team, with Jess doing all of the design work & James running the operation side of things (e.g glorified post man!)

Our cocker spaniel dog (Barley) is our official mascot & likes knocking things over with his over enthusiastic waggy tail

You may have seen some of our patterns & kits featured in a range of Cross Stitching Mags across the world as well as the craft Magazine 'Mollie Makes' In 2016 we won a competition with them for 'Best new Subscription Idea' in association with CrateJoy & this year we were also shortlisted for a Local Business award, which was pretty awesome!

All our kits & patterns are designed, packed up and shipped from our North Devon HQ & we are pretty sure that there is something in this book for everyone. (Unless you want to stitch up a vase of flowers or country cottage as that's not really our style!) as the patterns are easy to complete and all fit into a 4-6inch hoop, so perfectly sized projects (in our opinion!)

We really hope you love the patterns in this book, as much as we do. Please come check us out on social media as we love to chat stitching, dogs or anything unicorn ☺

Please note that all designs are for personal use only, so stitch em' up for your buds

Cross Stitching is so easy when you get the hang of it (and seriously pretty addictive!) you just need to learn a few basic steps & how to use your supplies correctly.

Here is a list of the items that you will need to complete the designs in this book, we will look into these in more detail so don't worry if you are a bit confused at first, it will all make perfect sense by the end ☺

If you already know how to cross stitch and are a seasoned pro, then please feel free to skip this section and go straight to the fun part (the patterns!)

Embroidery Hoop

WE RECOMMEND USING BAMBOO HOOPS AS THESE ARE MORE SUSTAINABLE

Wooden embroidery hoops are the most popular & come in a variety of different sizes (you will need a 4- 6 inch hoop for the patterns in this book) all hoops have a brass fixing at the top of the hoop which is used to tighten the material and secure it in place

Thread (or floss)

ALL PATTERNS IN THIS BOOK ARE TO BE STITCHED WITH 3 STRANDS OF THREAD

There are many different manufacturers of embroidery thread, however all our designs are based on using DMC threads. DMC are a French based company who are the market leaders in embroidery thread, which is 100% cotton. When Purchasing embroidery thread, you need to look out for 'Mouline Special 25' as this is the correct thickness of thread needed to complete the patterns. You will typically purchase 'Skeins' of 8M long thread, the thread itself is made up of 6 individual strands of cotton. All our patterns are based around using 3 strands, we will go into more detail on how to separate the threads further down the page

Material

ALL PATTERNS ARE TO BE STITCHED ON 14 COUNT AIDA OR 28 COUNT LINEN

The best material to cross stitch on is 'Aida' this is specially designed for cross stitching as it has lots of little holes, equally spaced across the fabric which means all your stitches will be the same size. Aida comes in different 'count' sizes; the count size is the number of squares per linear inch. The most popular size of aida is 14 count (this is what all are designs are based on) with count sizes, the higher the count, the smaller the stitches are.

Needle

The best types of needles to use for cross stitching are blunt tapestry needles (don't get them to sharp as it seriously hurts!) the size we recommend (and use for all our kits is 24)

♥ SETTING UP ♥

Once you have gathered up all your materials, you are ready to start stitching!
There are a couple of things you need to check before you start to make sure your finished piece looks ahhhmazing

1. Finding the centre of your Aida.

It is very important to make sure that you have a piece of material that is going to be big enough to complete the design (there is NOTHING worse than running out of material halfway through!) We always state the size needed to complete the pattern (plus some extra, just in case) to find the centre of your material, fold your material into four & draw a few lines (with a water soluble fabric pen) where the lines cross, later on you can gently wash these lines away in warm water once you have finished the design.

2. Preparing your hoop.

Once you have identified the centre of your piece of Aida & the correct sized hoop needed to complete the pattern, unscrew the brass fastening to its loosest setting. Next, place the largest half of the hoop over the material and the smallest half underneath the material. Stretch the larger hoop over the material and the smaller half of the hoop, making sure the material is straight. When you are happy with the positing of the material, tighten the brass fastening as tight as it will go, the material should be very taut & sound like a drum when you tap it (do a little dance to check if you like!)

3. Threading your needle

It's best to gather all the threads you need for the pattern before you begin. Each thread has a different number, these are listed in the pattern listing & are all DMC codes. When following cross stitch patterns its best to start in the middle of the design & work outwards, chose the thread which is closest to the centre of the pattern. Cut off a piece of thread around 30cm, next you need to carefully separate 3 strands of thread. Allow the thread to lay flat, with no twists (if your thread twists slightly then hold it out in front of you and allow the twists to fall out)

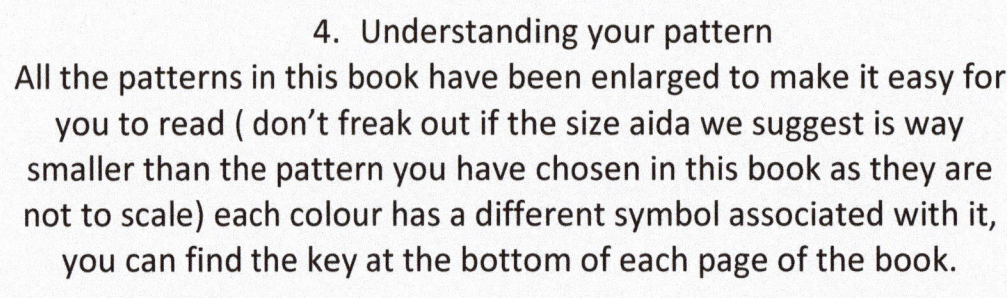

4. Understanding your pattern
All the patterns in this book have been enlarged to make it easy for you to read (don't freak out if the size aida we suggest is way smaller than the pattern you have chosen in this book as they are not to scale) each colour has a different symbol associated with it, you can find the key at the bottom of each page of the book.

So, now all the boring set up stuff if out the way we can come onto the fun part of how to actually cross stitch & to be honest its actually super easy, like just making a cross with thread kinda easy!

- You will notice that your pattern contains a lot of different symbols (don't worry these are supposed to be there!) each pattern is made up of a number of different symbols which represent the different coloured threads. You just need to match up your thread colour with the symbol & then you are pretty much good to go!

- Using an embroidery hoop will make your life 100% easier – we recommend bamboo hoops as these are a lot more sustainable then regular wooden hoops (as bamboo grows hella' fast compared to normal trees) firstly you need to undo the brass fastenings, so you have two separate halves

- Get your piece of material (14 count aida is best for all our projects) and fold into four, where the two lines cross is the centre of your project

- Place your material as central as you can (use your folds as guidance) between the two halves of the hoop and tighten the metal fastening, your fabric should be tight and sounds like a drum (do a little happy dance to test!)

- All patterns are stitched with three strands of embroidery thread (we use DMC but there are loads of other brands available, but

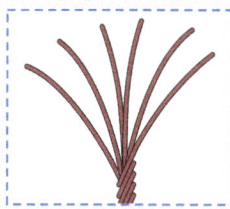

our patterns use the DMC thread colours) You will notice that your thread skeins have 6 strands. You need to cut a length of around 30cm and then gently split your thread into two – if you have problems splitting your thread you can roll the thread between your fingers and it will come away from itself

- With cross stitching its best to stitch from the middle, outwards (otherwise

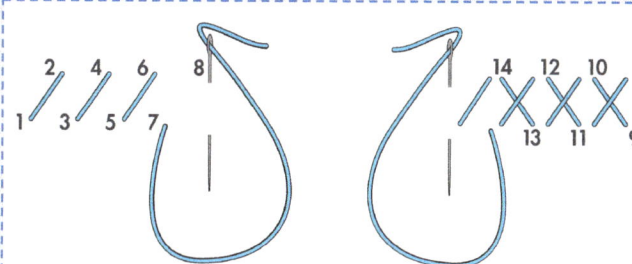

you may run out of material and this is the worst thing ever) on the pattern there will be two red lines, where they cross is the middle of the pattern & the first thread colour you will use

- Now you need to get your needle, select the thread colour that your need, cut a length of thread (approx. 30cm) and separate the strands, tie a small knot on one end and then thread the loose end through the eye of the needle. Use this method every time you need to change thread colours.
- Now it's time to start stitching! A good tip is to try and keep your stitches in the same direction, so they end up looking super neat. Start from the underside of the material (coming up at number 1) and go to the opposite corner (number 2) then from the underside go up to position three then to position 4 and just repeat! You then need to come back in the opposite direction (starting at position 9)
- Sometimes it may be easier to stitch the individual crosses in one go. Starting in the same way but instead, when you get to position 3, go to the hole which is the left of position 2. You have completed one stitch! Go back to position 3 and repeat.
- Back stitch is demonstrated as a coloured line on the pattern. Firstly, make a single straight stitch (starting at the underside of position 1) continue along the pattern but come up the space ahead & bring your

needle back down in the same hole at the end of the last stitch you made.
- Once you have completed your design, remove from the hoop (wash gently in warm water if you like) and then iron (the underside) you can then reposition your design in the hoop and trim off any excess material.

♥ PATTERNS ♥

Now onto the fun part!
You will find over 30 of our fave patterns which are split into sections – there is everything from florals, to rainbows & animal friends. All patterns in this book are stitched in either a 4,5 or 6 inch hoop, on 14 count aida and with 3 strands of DMC thread.

There is backstitch in some of the patterns, which looks better if you use 2 strands of thread, but it totes up to you which you prefer! There are 7 new and totally exclusive patterns in this book as well as some of our bestselling designs. Enjoy!

THE SUNFLOWER GARDEN

stitch me
in a 6 inch hoop
on 14 count aida
size 20cm x 20cm

	Number	Name:	Strands	Estimated Length	Stitches
X	DMC 310	Black	3	27.3 cm	8
C	DMC 747	Blue Sky V LT	3	203.2 cm	113
N	DMC 975	Brown Golden DK	3	167.2 cm	74
⊘	DMC 554	Violet LT	3	107.9 cm	60
O	DMC 3348	Yellow Green LT	3	188.8 cm	105
♠	DMC 3347	Yellow Green Med	3	305.7 cm	170
b	DMC 3346	Hunter Green Med	3	215.8 cm	120
↓	DMC 894	Carnation V LT	3	75.5 cm	42
♠	DMC 893	Carnation LT	3	32.4 cm	18
Z	DMC 307	Lemon	3	341.7 cm	190
◤	DMC 444	Lemon DK	3	18.8 cm	6
N	DMC 976	Brown Golden MD	3	37.8 cm	21
≡	DMC 208	Lavender V DK	3	32.4 cm	18

IT WILL BE OK

stitch me
in a 6 inch hoop
on 14 count aida
size 20cm x 20cm

	Number	Name:	Strands	Estimated Length	Stitches
	DMC 310	Black	3	510.9 cm	158
	DMC 208	Lavender V DK	3	89.9 cm	50
	DMC 554	Violet LT	3	377.6 cm	210
	DMC 307	Lemon	3	50.4 cm	28
	DMC 015	Avocado Green Ultra	3	609.6 cm	339
	DMC 718	Plum	3	98.9 cm	55
	DMC 033	Plum	3	47.5 cm	12
	DMC 907	Green Parrot LT	3	414.7 cm	227

HANG ON, LET ME OVERTHINK THIS

stitch me
in a 6 inch hoop
on 14 count aida
size 20cm x 20cm

	Number	Name:	Strands	Estimated Length	Stitches
◖	DMC 907	Green Parrot LT	3	879.4 cm	489
✖	DMC 208	Lavender V DK	3	1147.3 cm	638
b	DMC 307	Lemon	3	250.0 cm	139
▣	DMC 898	Brown Coffee V DK	3	48.6 cm	27
☐	DMC 310	Black	3	352.0 cm	0
●	DMC 893	Carnation LT	3	661.8 cm	368

UGH, PEOPLE

stitch me
in a 6 inch hoop
on 14 count aida
size 20cm x 20cm

	Number	Name:	Strands	Estimated Length	Stitches
▢	DMC 310	Black	3	185.5 cm	0
✖	DMC 015	Yellow Green LT	3	136.7 cm	76
◉	DMC 907	Green Parrot LT	3	503.5 cm	280
↓	DMC 894	Carnation V LT	3	82.7 cm	46
▲	DMC 893	Carnation LT	3	176.2 cm	98
Z	DMC 445	Lemon LT	3	287.7 cm	160
▣	DMC 208	Lavender V DK	3	91.7 cm	51
♣	DMC 554	Violet LT	3	84.5 cm	47
⊟	DMC 307	Lemon	3	115.1 cm	64

YOU CAN NEVER HAVE TOO MANY PLANTS

stitch me

in a 6 inch hoop

on 14 count aida

size 20cm x 20cm

YOU CAN NEVER HAVE TOO MANY PLANTS

	Number	Name:	Strands	Estimated Length	Stitches
	DMC 310	Black	3	108.6 cm	0
	DMC 3773	Flesh Med	3	111.5 cm	62
Σ	DMC 3348	Yellow Green LT	3	301.8 cm	165
	DMC 907	Green Parrot LT	3	327.7 cm	178
b	DMC 702	Kelly Green	3	134.6 cm	62
i	DMC 211	Lavender LT	3	196.0 cm	109
	DMC 209	Lavender DK	3	18.0 cm	10
—	DMC 747	Blue Sky V LT	3	194.2 cm	108
a	DMC 3846	Turquoise Bright LT	3	18.0 cm	10
c	DMC 894	Carnation V LT	3	120.5 cm	67
▲	DMC 445	Lemon LT	3	210.4 cm	117
W	DMC 444	Lemon DK	3	18.0 cm	10
	DMC 602	Cranberry MD	3	30.6 cm	17

LIFE IS SHORT, BUY THE PLANTS

stitch me
in a 6 inch hoop
on 14 count aida
size 20cm x 20cm

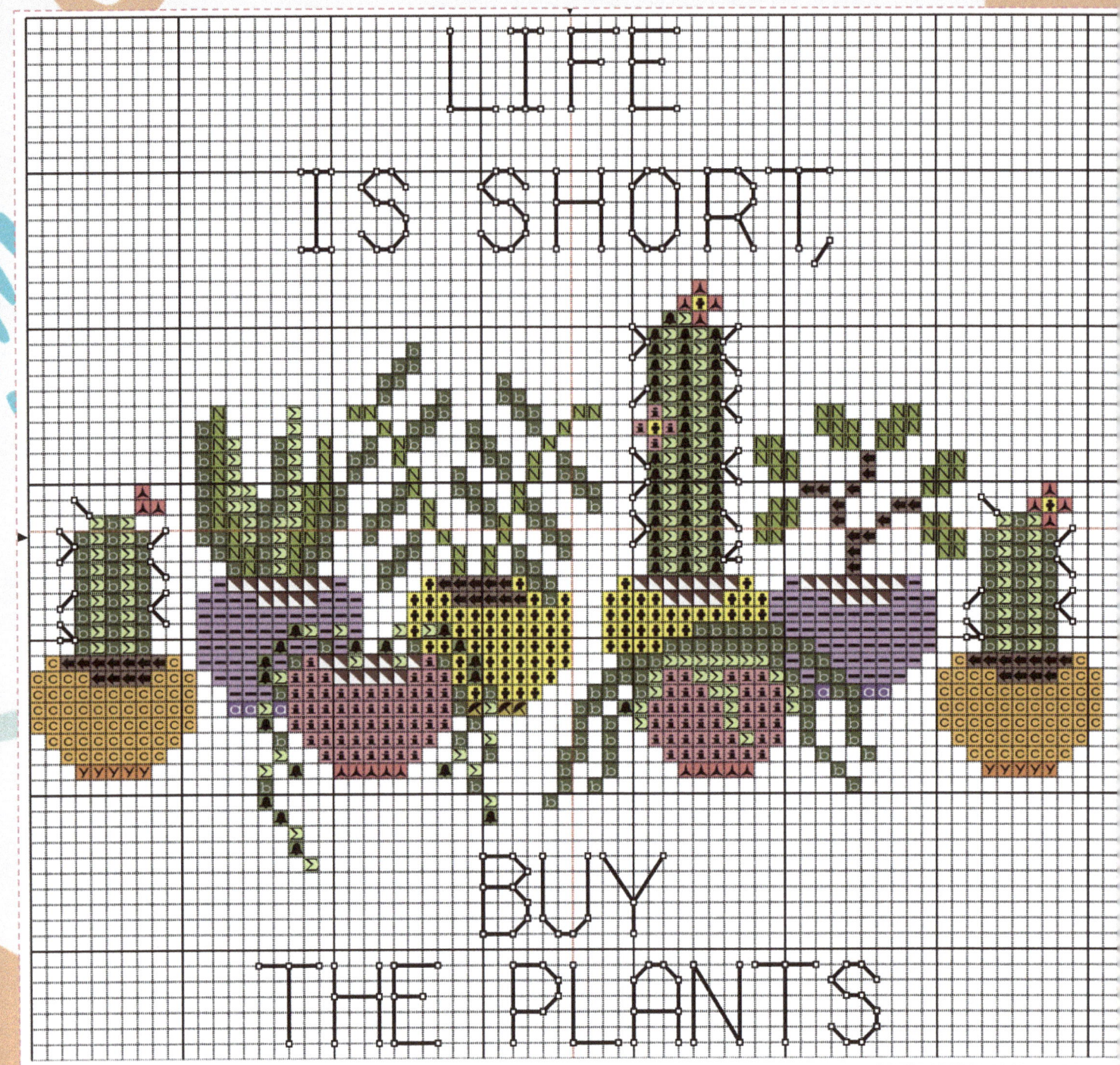

	Number	Name:	Strands	Estimated Length	Stitches
✖	DMC 310	Black	3	452.9 cm	0
◥	DMC 3772	Flesh VY DK	3	77.3 cm	43
◀	DMC 3773	Flesh Med	3	82.7 cm	46
Σ	DMC 3348	Yellow Green LT	3	228.4 cm	127
▲	DMC 3347	Yellow Green Med	3	115.1 cm	64
b	DMC 3346	Hunter Green Med	3	386.6 cm	215
▲	DMC 893	Carnation LT	3	37.8 cm	21
◤	DMC 444	Lemon DK	3	5.4 cm	3
i	DMC 894	Carnation V LT	3	185.2 cm	103
♣	DMC 307	Lemon	3	154.7 cm	86
▬	DMC 554	Violet LT	3	174.4 cm	97
a	DMC 208	Lavender V DK	3	10.8 cm	6
C	DMC 742	Tangerine LT	3	208.6 cm	116
Y	DMC 740	Tangerine	3	18.0 cm	10
N	DMC 907	Green Parrot LT	3	163.6 cm	91

BE A RAINBOW

BE A RAINBOW IN SOMEONE ELSE'S CLOUD

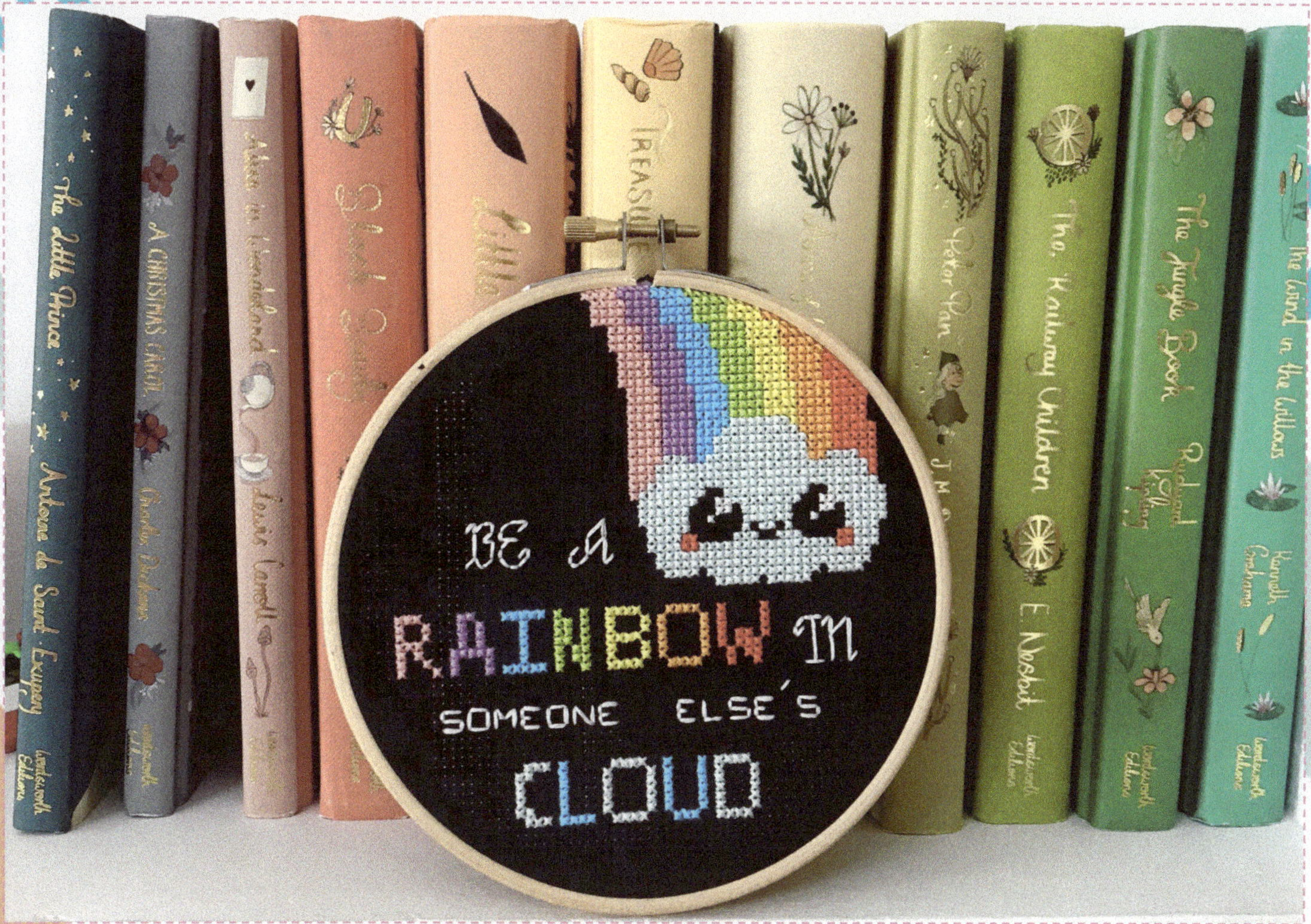

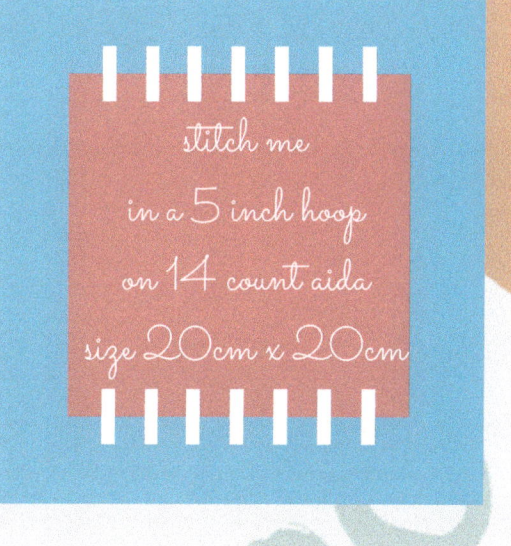

TOP TIP!
WHEN STITCHING ON BLACK FABRIC PLACE A PIECE OF WHITE PAPER ON YOUR LAP

stitch me
in a 5 inch hoop
on 14 count aida
size 20cm x 20cm

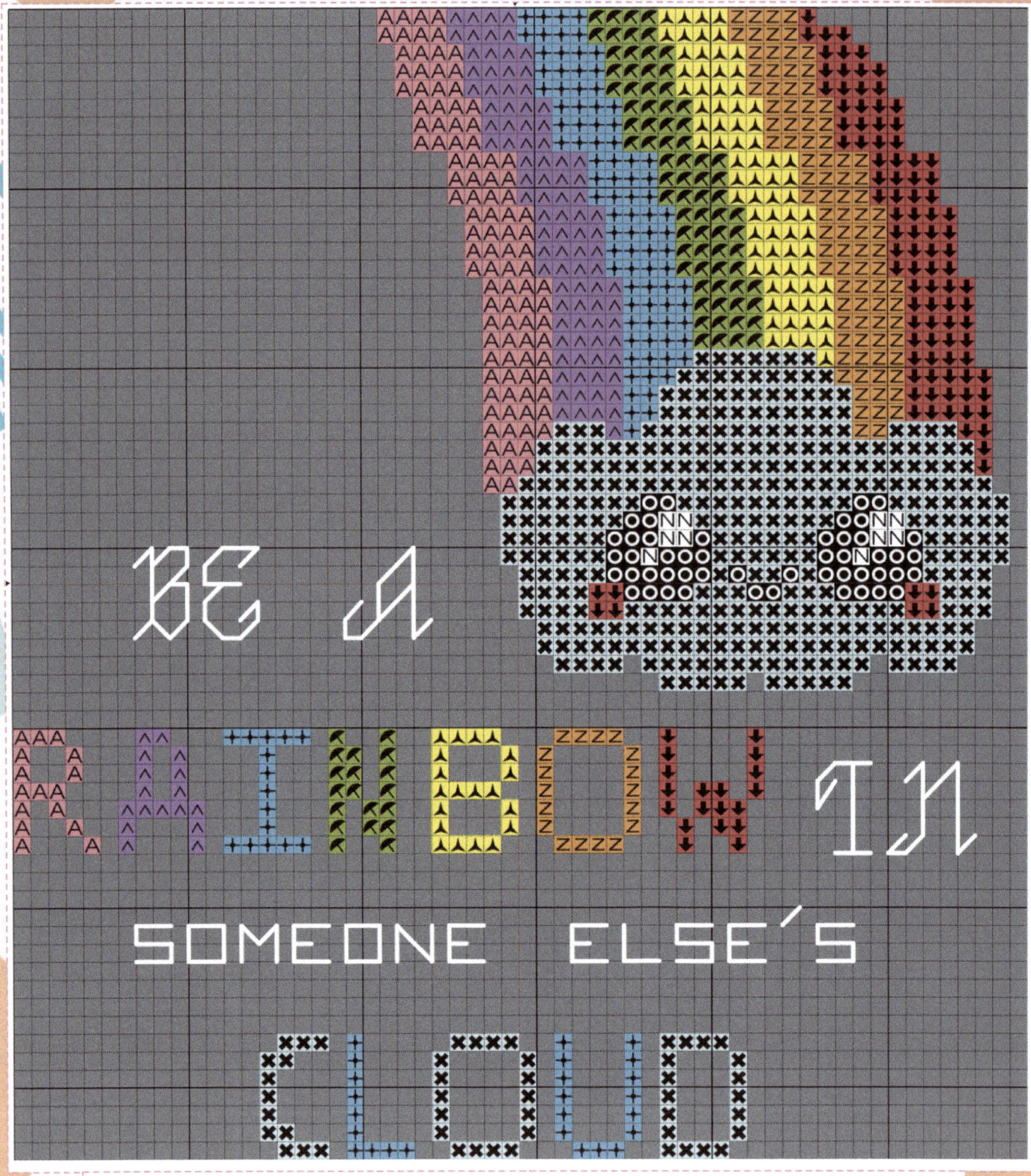

	Number	Name:	Strands	Estimated Length	Stitches
O	DMC 310	Black	3	89.9 cm	50
N	DMC BLANC	White	3	263.6 cm	10
X	DMC 747	Blue Sky V LT	3	706.7 cm	393
∧	DMC 209	Lavender DK	3	197.8 cm	110
↓	DMC 3801	Melon V DK	3	217.6 cm	121
⅄	DMC 307	Lemon	3	174.4 cm	97
✛	DMC 3845	Turquoise Bright MD	3	230.2 cm	128
A	DMC 894	Carnation V LT	3	215.8 cm	120
Z	DMC 741	Tangerine MD	3	197.8 cm	110
◤	DMC 907	Green Parrot LT	3	170.8 cm	95

BE A RAINBOW

YOU CAN'T HAVE A RAINBOW WITHOUT THE RAIN

stitch me
in a 6 inch hoop
on 14 count aida
size 20cm x 20cm

	Number	Name:	Strands	Estimated Length	Stitches
N	DMC 5200	White Bright (B5200)	3	7.2 cm	4
∧	DMC 209	Lavender DK	3	118.7 cm	66
✦	DMC 740	Tangerine	3	223.0 cm	124
▬	DMC 3801	Melon V DK	3	383.0 cm	213
ƹ	DMC 307	Lemon	3	194.2 cm	108
W	DMC 907	Green Parrot LT	3	210.4 cm	117
∩	DMC 747	Blue Sky V LT	3	456.8 cm	254
◑	DMC 3846	Turquoise Bright LT	3	521.5 cm	290
◒	DMC 3608	Plum V LT	3	97.1 cm	54
◪	DMC 310	Black	3	212.4 cm	44

'TIS THE SEASON

OH DEER, CHRISTMAS IS HERE

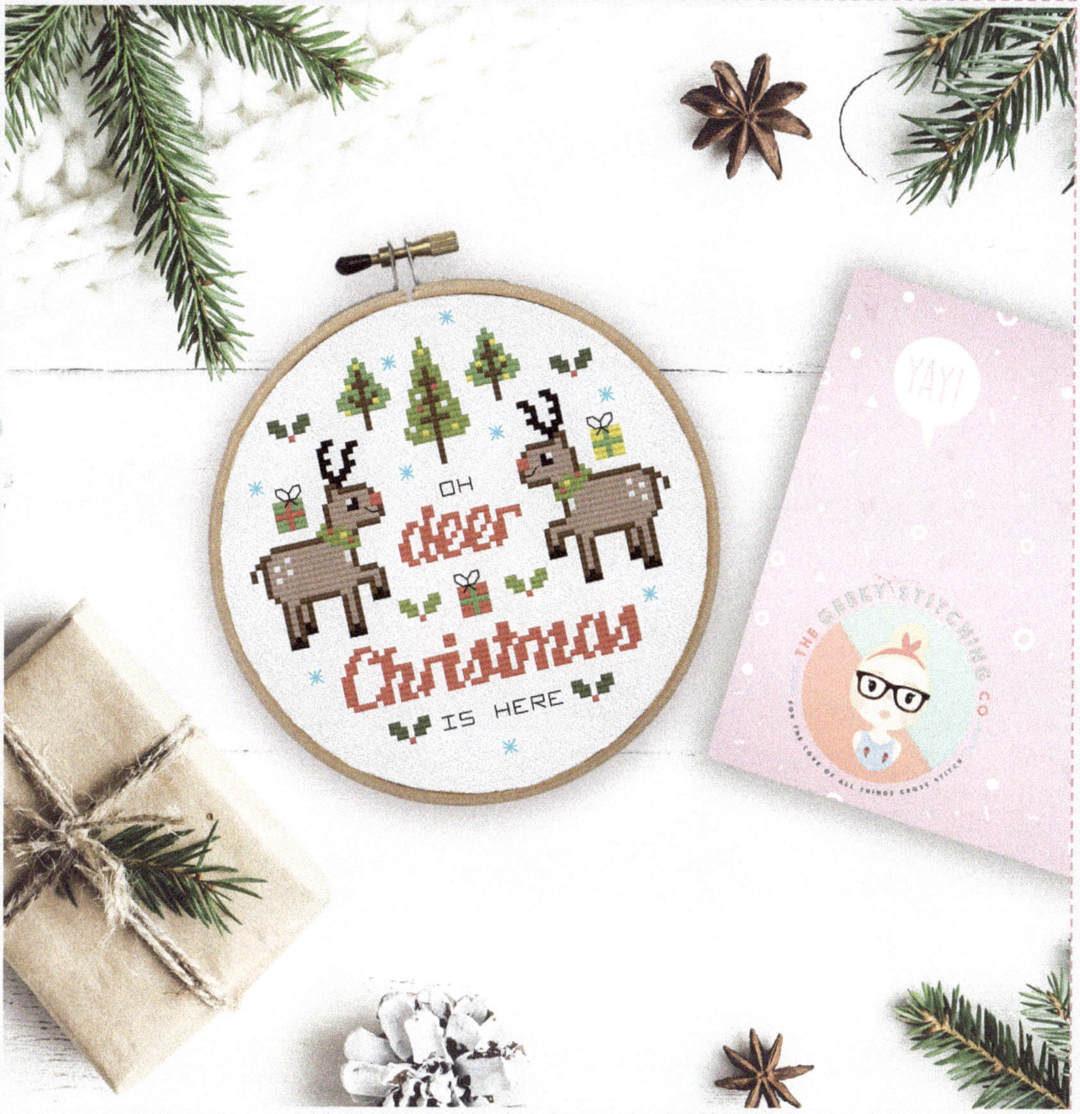

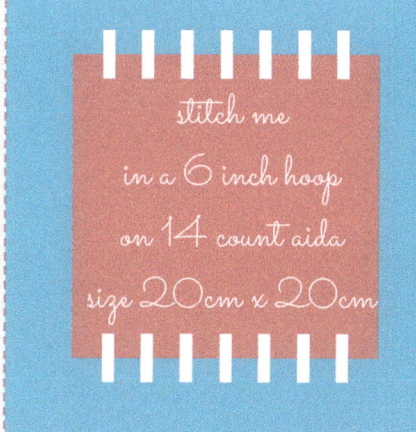

stitch me
in a 6 inch hoop
on 14 count aida
size 20cm x 20cm

	Number	Name:	Strands	Estimated Length	Stitches
▲	DMC 310	Black	3	198.4 cm	82
N	DMC 5200	White Bright (B5200)	3	30.6 cm	17
⊙	DMC 3864	Mocha Beige LT	3	571.9 cm	318
✖	DMC 3862	Mocha Beige DK	3	438.8 cm	244
ⓘ	DMC 3846	Turquoise Bright LT	3	41.0 cm	0
▬	DMC 307	Lemon	3	53.9 cm	30
◫	DMC 907	Green Parrot LT	3	246.4 cm	137
▣	DMC 3346	Hunter Green Med	3	100.7 cm	56
◀	DMC 703	Chartreuse	3	174.4 cm	97
2	DMC 3801	Melon V DK	3	622.2 cm	346

'TIS THE SEASON

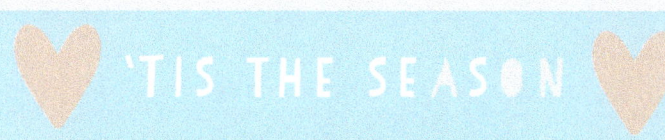

'TIS THE SEASON

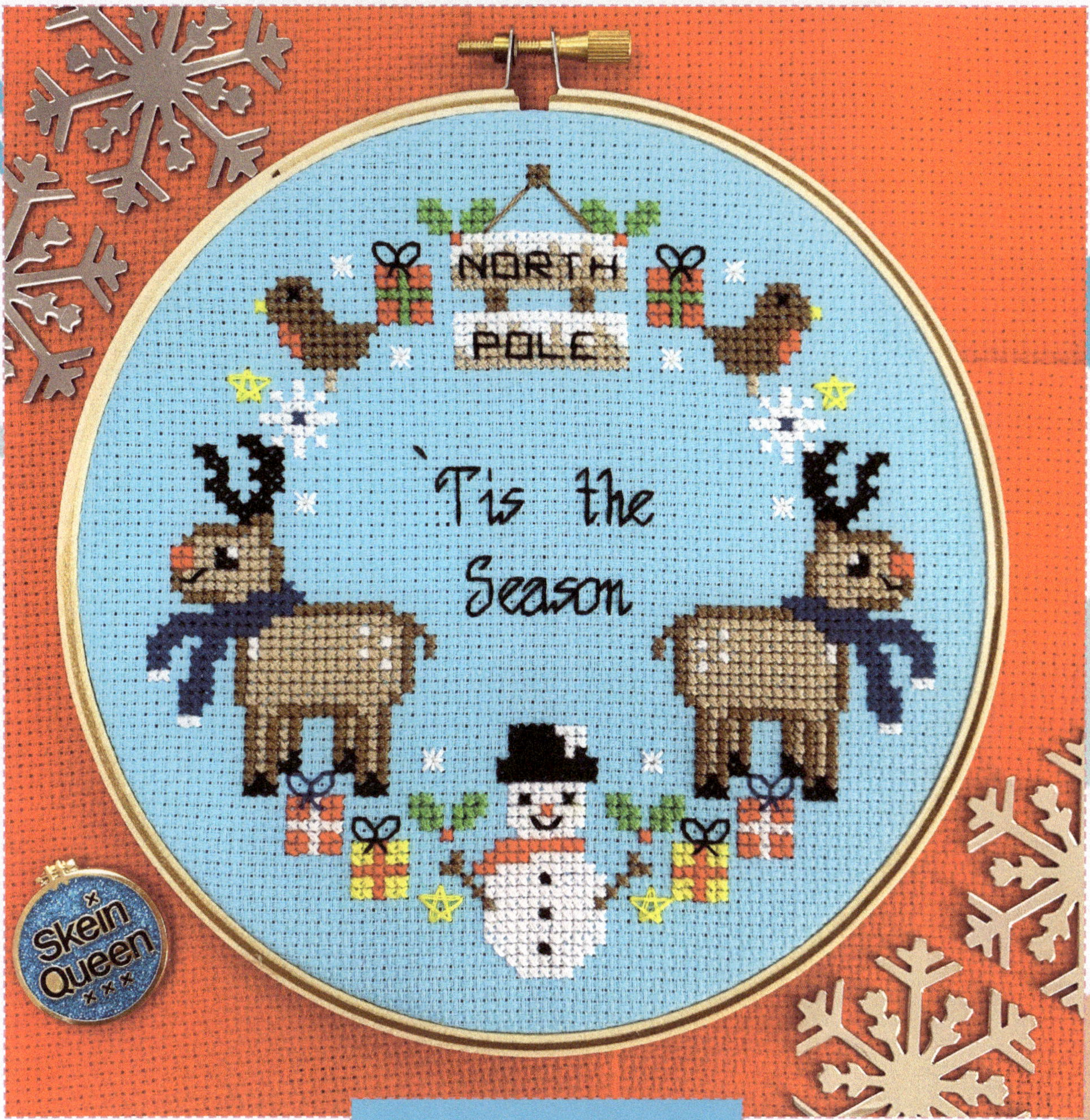
NORTH
POLE
'Tis the Season
Skein Queen

stitch me
in a 6 inch hoop
on 14 count aida
size 20cm x 20cm

	Number	Name:	Strands	Estimated Length	Stitches
	DMC 310	Black	3	877.6 cm	130
	DMC 3771	Terracotta Ultra V LT	3	737.3 cm	410
	DMC 3801	Christmas Red LT	3	208.6 cm	116
	DMC 3772	Flesh VY DK	3	518.5 cm	284
	DMC BLANC	White	3	582.0 cm	278
	DMC 307	Lemon	3	184.9 cm	35
	DMC 702	Kelly Green	3	182.1 cm	74
	DMC 311	Blue Navy MD	3	250.6 cm	111

'TIS THE SEASON

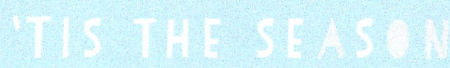

DACHSHUND THROUGH THE SNOW

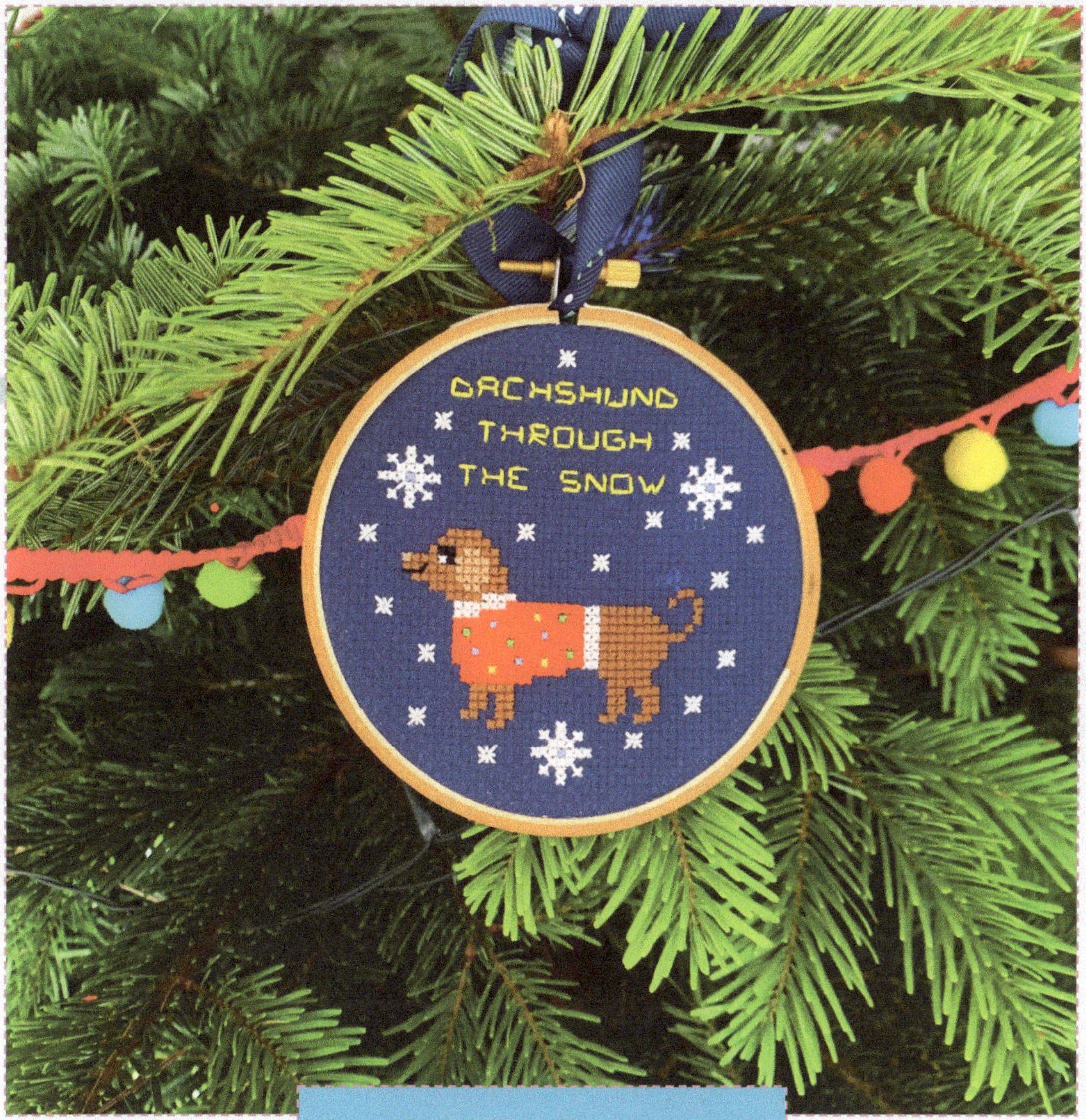

stitch me
in a 4 inch hoop
on 14 count aida
size 15cm x 15cm

	Number	Name:	Strands	Estimated Length	Stitches
✖	DMC 310	Black	3	43.8 cm	4
N	DMC BLANC	White	3	294.9 cm	88
◆	DMC 3801	Christmas Red LT	3	188.8 cm	105
●	DMC 3864	Mocha Beige LT	3	28.8 cm	16
⊙	DMC 3862	Mocha Beige DK	3	273.3 cm	152
▬	DMC 156	Blue Violet MD LT	3	12.6 cm	7
⊞	DMC 307	Lemon	3	152.6 cm	3
C	DMC 702	Kelly Green	3	7.2 cm	4

NOT ALL HEROES WEAR CAPES

stitch me
in a 6 inch hoop
on 14 count aida
size 20cm x 20cm

	Number	Name:	Strands	Estimated Length	Stitches
✖	DMC 310	Black	3	1042.3 cm	342
N	DMC 5200	White Bright (B5200)	3	7.2 cm	4
Σ	DMC 3348	Yellow Green LT	3	179.8 cm	100
▲	DMC 3347	Yellow Green Med	3	71.9 cm	40
★	DMC 975	Golden Brown DK	3	110.4 cm	44
ℹ	DMC 156	Blue Violet MD LT	3	355.7 cm	114
▽	DMC 157	Blue Cornflower V LT	3	640.2 cm	356
O	DMC 307	Lemon	3	532.3 cm	296
a	DMC 3708	Melon LT	3	194.2 cm	108
S	DMC 907	Green Parrot LT	3	215.8 cm	120
●	DMC 554	Violet LT	3	140.3 cm	78

I'D RATHER BE SLEEPING

stitch me
in a 6 inch hoop
on 14 count aida
size 20cm x 20cm

	Number	Name:	Strands	Estimated Length	Stitches
	DMC 975	Brown Golden DK	3	479.3 cm	253
	DMC 3771	Terracotta Ultra V LT	3	378.7 cm	205
	DMC 3773	Desert Sand MD	3	2273.1 cm	1264
2	DMC 603	Cranberry	3	57.5 cm	32
	DMC 310	Black	3	1179.3 cm	559
N	DMC 703	Chartreuse	3	160.7 cm	70

stitch me
in a 6 inch hoop
on 14 count aida
size 20cm x 20cm

	Number	Name:	Strands	Estimated Length	Stitches
☒	DMC 310	Black	3	203.4 cm	48
◄	DMC B5200	Snow White	3	199.6 cm	111
⊙	DMC 986	Green Forest V DK	3	402.8 cm	224
▣	DMC 3855	Autumn Gold LT	3	152.9 cm	85
Y	DMC 3801	Melon V DK	3	89.9 cm	50
◖	DMC 741	Tangerine MD	3	230.2 cm	128
▽	DMC 947	Burnt Orange	3	679.8 cm	378
▲	DMC 702	Kelly Green	3	194.2 cm	108

FURRY FRIENDS

FLUFFY RED ROBIN

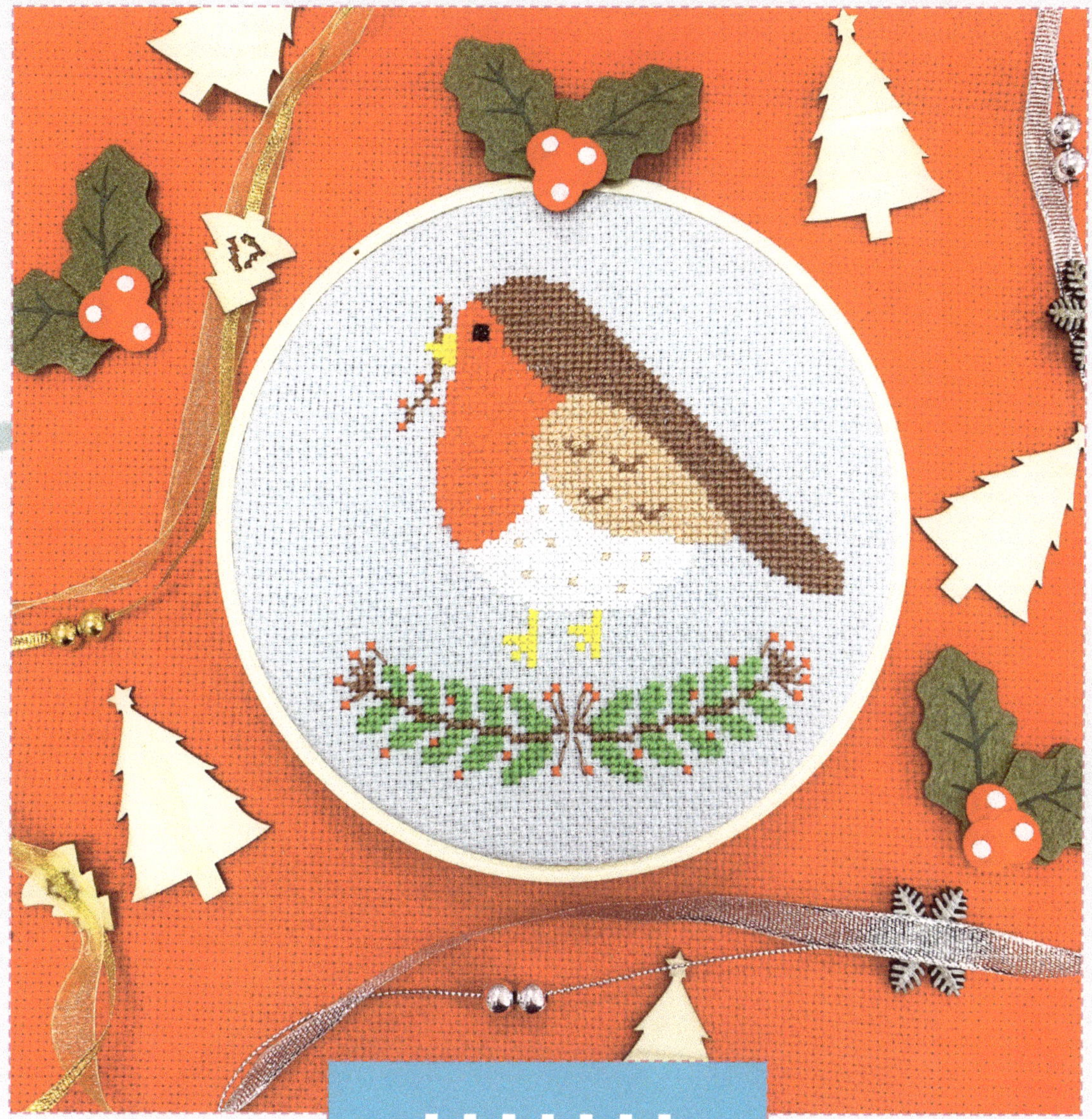

stitch me
in a 6 inch hoop
on 14 count aida
size 20cm x 20cm

	Number	Name:	Strands	Estimated Length	Stitches
Y	DMC 310	Black	3	7.2 cm	4
C	DMC 3772	Desert Sand V DK	3	852.5 cm	445
b	DMC 702	Kelly Green	3	456.8 cm	254
C	DMC 3771	Terracotta Ultra V LT	3	487.3 cm	271
O	DMC BLANC	White	3	440.6 cm	245
2	DMC 444	Lemon DK	3	61.1 cm	34
Σ	DMC 3801	Melon V DK	3	584.5 cm	325
N	DMC 975	Brown Golden DK"	3	118.7 cm	66

TOTALLY JAWSOME

stitch me
in a 6 inch hoop
on 14 count aida
size 20cm x 20cm

	Number	Name:	Strands	Estimated Length	Stitches
■	DMC 156	Blue Violet MD LT	3	1918.8 cm	1067
⚐	DMC 157	Blue Cornflower V LT	3	528.7 cm	294
✖	DMC 310	Black	3	877.4 cm	460
■	DMC BLANC	White	3	226.6 cm	126

FOOD, FUN & PUNS

LIVIN' LIFE ON THE VEG

stitch me
in a 6 inch hoop
on 14 count aida
size 20cm x 20cm

	Number	Name:	Strands	Estimated Length	Stitches
E	DMC 310	Black	3	381.8 cm	73
C	DMC 3801	Melon V DK	3	194.2 cm	108
◣	DMC 904	Green Parrot V DK	3	949.5 cm	528
✦	DMC 208	Lavender V DK	3	634.8 cm	353
❜	DMC 605	Cranberry V LT	3	89.9 cm	50
★	DMC 947	Burnt Orange	3	566.5 cm	315
☾	DMC 703	Chartreuse	3	464.0 cm	258
■	DMC 741	Tangerine MD	3	52.2 cm	29
Ⲏ	DMC 702	Kelly Green	3	120.5 cm	67
N	DMC B5200	Snow White	3	30.6 cm	17

SQUEEZE THE DAY

stitch me
in a 4 inch hoop
on 14 count aida
size 15cm x 15cm

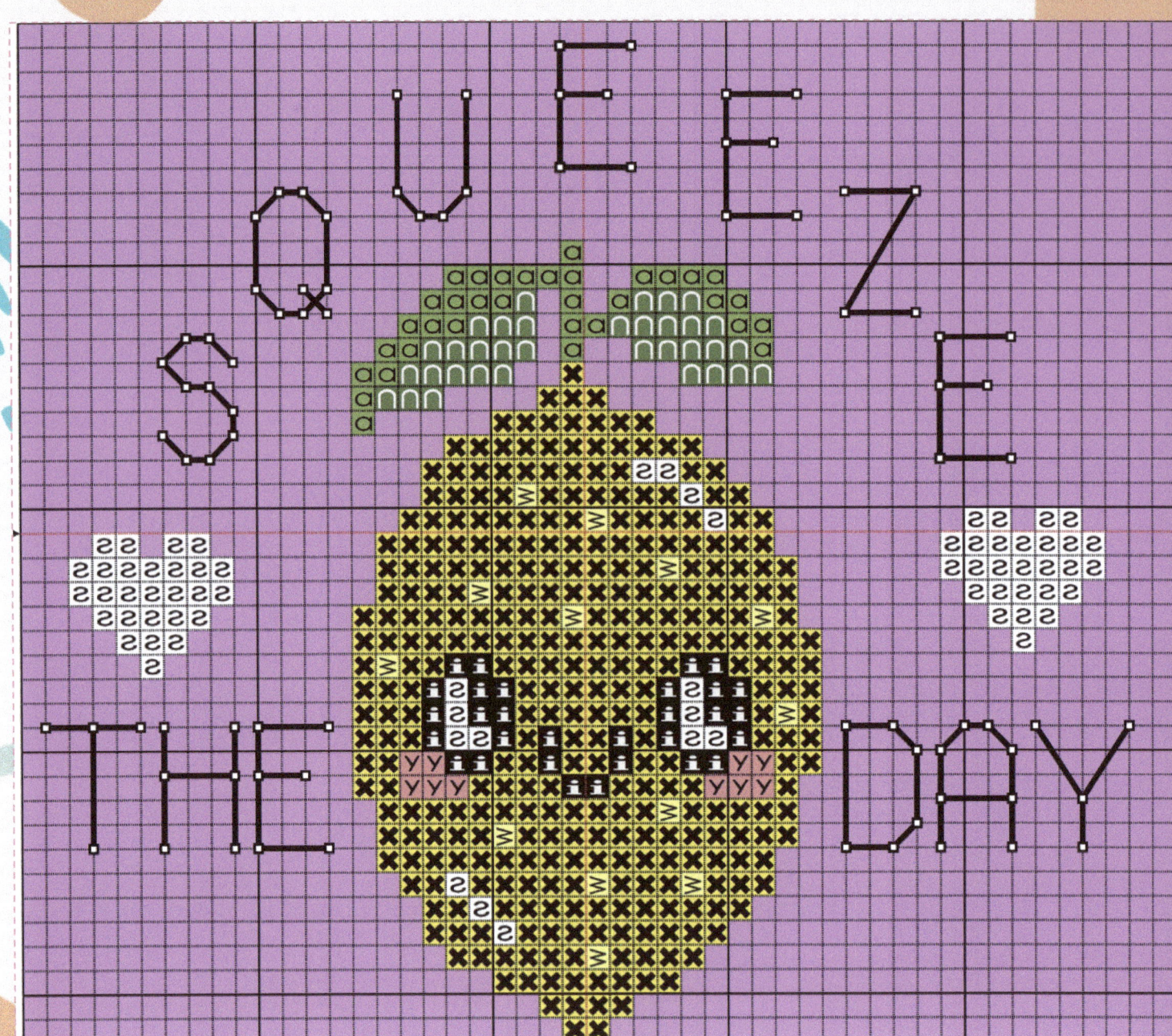

	Number	Name:	Strands	Estimated Length	Stitches
i	DMC 310	Black	3	131.4 cm	30
X	DMC 307	Lemon	3	591.6 cm	329
a	DMC 703	Chartreuse	3	61.1 cm	34
y	DMC 894	Carnation V LT	3	18.0 cm	10
s	DMC B5200	Snow White	3	124.1 cm	69
w	DMC 445	Lemon LT	3	23.4 cm	13
n	DMC 702	Kelly Green	3	61.1 cm	34

FOOD, FUN & PUNS

THE ORIGINAL BREAKFAST CLUB

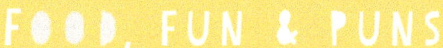

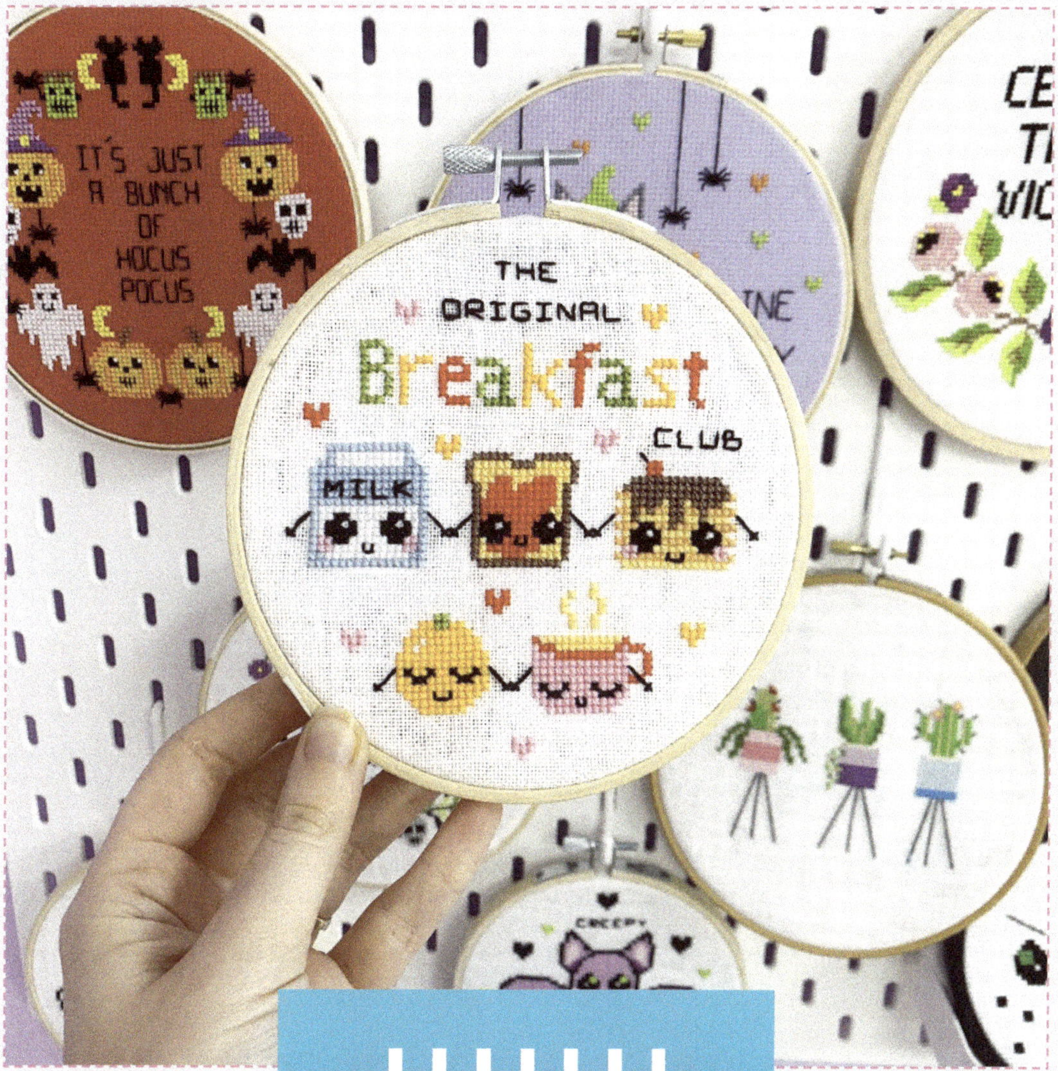

stitch me
in a 5 inch hoop
on 14 count aida
size 20cm x 20cm

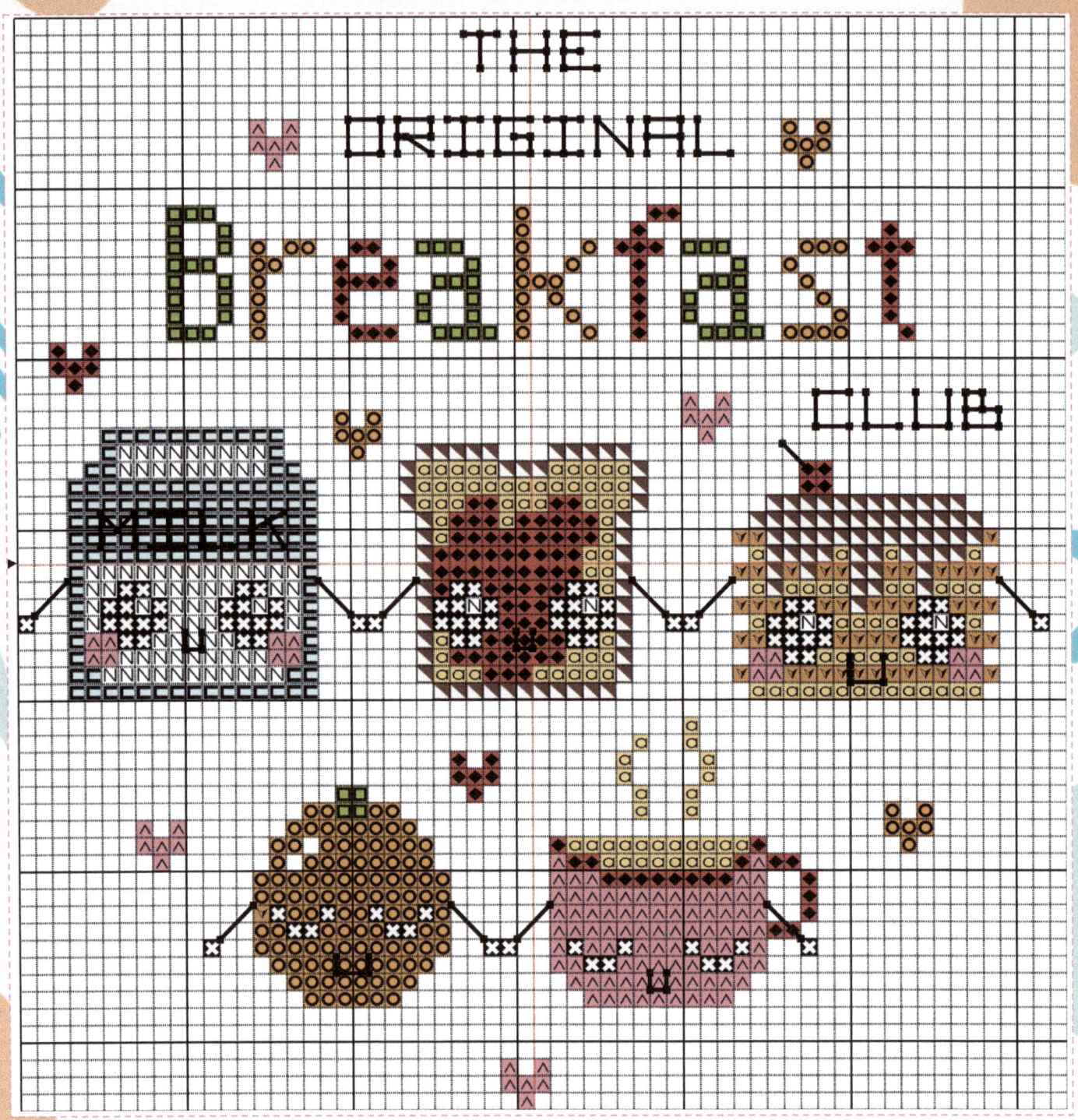

	Number	Name:	Strands	Estimated Length	Stitches
□	DMC 310	Black	3	417.9 cm	92
N	DMC 5200	White Bright (B5200)	3	147.5 cm	82
ᴇ	DMC 747	Blue Sky V LT	3	219.4 cm	122
◆	DMC 3801	Christmas Red LT	3	246.4 cm	137
◣	DMC 3772	Flesh VY DK	3	196.0 cm	109
∧	DMC 894	Carnation V LT	3	223.0 cm	124
Y	DMC 977	Golden Brown LT	3	82.7 cm	46
ᴀ	DMC 3855	Autumn Gold LT	3	223.0 cm	124
▣	DMC 907	Green Parrot LT	3	95.3 cm	53
◉	DMC 741	Tangerine MD	3	284.1 cm	158

 # LOVE THE EARTH

THERE IS NO PLANET B

stitch me
in a 6 inch hoop
on 14 count aida
size 20cm x 20cm

	Number	Name:	Strands	Estimated Length	Stitches
O	DMC 310	Black	3	648.8 cm	36
N	DMC 5200	White Bright (B5200)	3	18.0 cm	10
3	DMC 3855	Autumn Gold LT	3	223.0 cm	124
←	DMC 156	Blue Violet MD LT	3	282.3 cm	157
Y	DMC 977	Golden Brown LT	3	28.8 cm	16
★	DMC 975	Golden Brown DK	3	351.0 cm	177
▽	DMC 002	Pearl Gray V LT	3	125.1 cm	62
I	DMC 414	Steel Gray DK	3	153.8 cm	84
i	DMC 894	Carnation V LT	3	71.1 cm	35
—	DMC 740	Tangerine	3	74.8 cm	34
a	DMC 742	Tangerine LT	3	77.1 cm	41
Y	DMC 307	Lemon	3	79.6 cm	43
✖	DMC 031	Blue Violet MD LT	3	350.0 cm	194
∩	DMC 157	Blue Cornflower V LT	3	229.5 cm	127
●	DMC 907	Green Parrot LT	3	360.6 cm	199
▣	DMC 3773	Desert Sand MD	3	51.7 cm	24

LOVE THE EARTH

stitch me
in a 6 inch hoop
on 14 count aida
size 20cm x 20cm

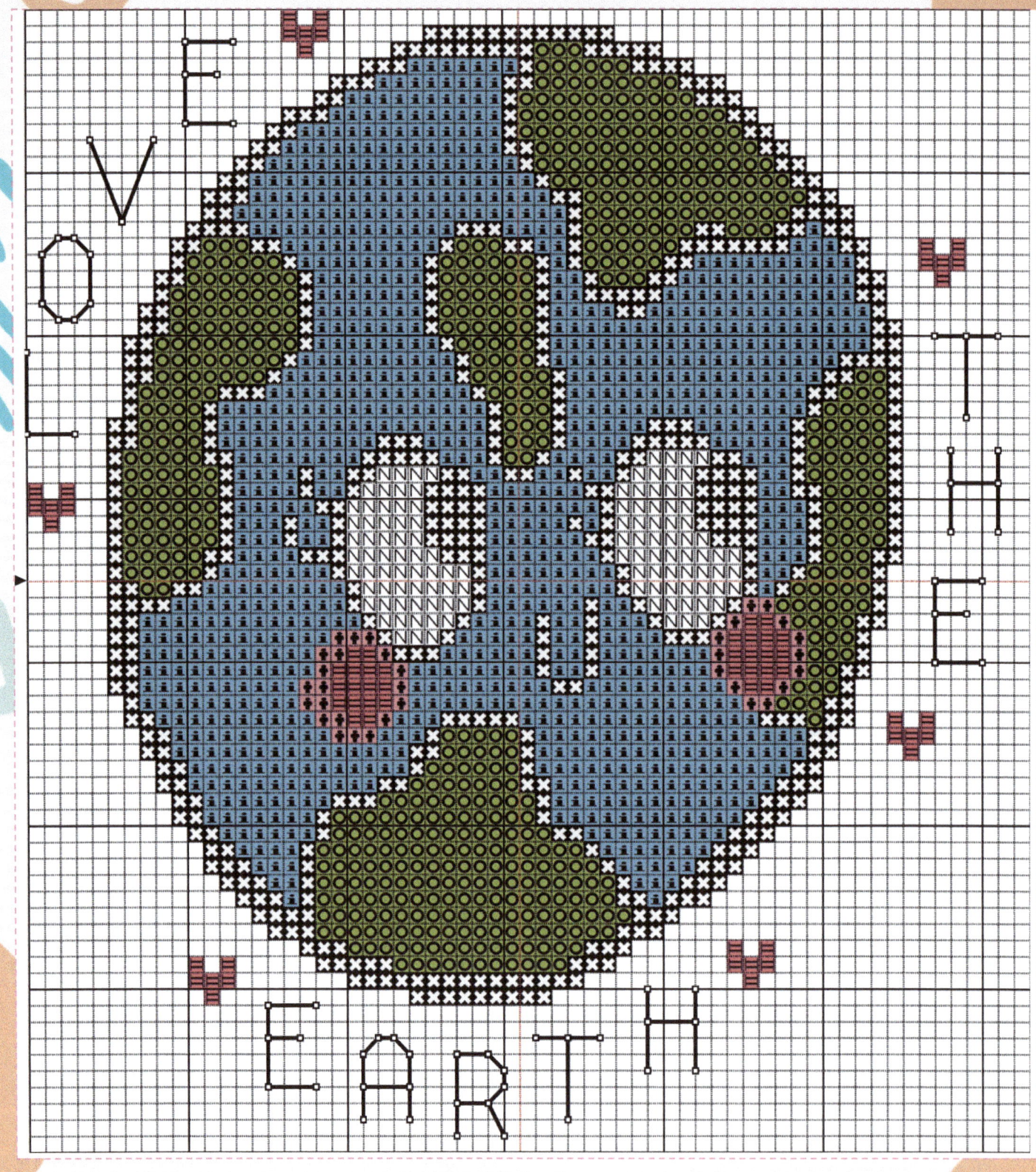

	Number	Name:	Strands	Estimated Length	Stitches
✖	DMC 310	Black	3	1238.0 cm	555
⚑	DMC 3845	Turquoise Bright MD	3	1832.5 cm	1019
✿	DMC 894	Carnation V LT	3	61.1 cm	34
◉	DMC 907	Green Parrot LT	3	1116.8 cm	621
N	DMC B5200	Snow White	3	212.2 cm	118
☷	DMC 893	Carnation LT	3	122.3 cm	68

PUMPKIN SPICE SEASON

AUTUMN LEAVES

stitch me

in a 6 inch hoop

on 14 count aida

size 20cm x 20cm

	Number	Name:	Strands	Estimated Length	Stitches
✖	DMC 310	Black	3	71.9 cm	40
👤	DMC 605	Cranberry V LT	3	106.1 cm	59
▣	DMC 947	Burnt Orange	3	287.7 cm	160
⬤	DMC 3801	Christmas Red LT	3	836.2 cm	465
∧	DMC B5200	Snow White	3	1065.2 cm	517
▽	DMC 726	Topaz LT	3	185.2 cm	103
▬	DMC 975	Golden Brown DK	3	159.0 cm	83
▲	DMC 741	Tangerine MD	3	205.0 cm	114
◆	DMC 444	Lemon DK	3	111.5 cm	62
■	DMC 445	Lemon LT	3	106.1 cm	59

PUMPKIN SPICE SEASON

PUMPKIN SPICE & ALL THINGS NICE

stitch me
in a 6 inch hoop
on 14 count aida
size 20cm x 20cm

	Number	Name:	Strands	Estimated Length	Stitches
	DMC 310	Black	3	97.1 cm	54
N	DMC 5200	White Bright (B5200)	3	10.8 cm	6
	DMC 977	Brown Golden LT	3	71.9 cm	40
	DMC 3801	Christmas Red LT	3	264.4 cm	147
	DMC 975	Golden Brown DK	3	126.6 cm	63
	DMC 740	Tangerine	3	951.3 cm	529
	DMC 742	Tangerine LT	3	902.8 cm	502

AUTUMN LEAVES & PUMPKINS PLEASE

stitch me
in a 6 inch hoop
on 14 count aida
size 20cm x 20cm

	Number	Name:	Strands	Estimated Length	Stitches
✖	DMC 310	Black	3	122.3 cm	68
▽	DMC 976	Brown Golden MD	3	1413.5 cm	786
●	DMC 742	Tangerine LT	3	1129.3 cm	628
▲	DMC 975	Brown Golden DK	3	908.2 cm	505
∧	DMC 726	Topaz LT	3	636.6 cm	354
N	DMC 3801	Melon V DK	3	622.2 cm	346
⊟	DMC 947	Burnt Orange	3	125.9 cm	70
☐	DMC B5200	Snow White	3	16.2 cm	9

BRAND NEW PATTERNS

ALWAYS BEE YOURSELF

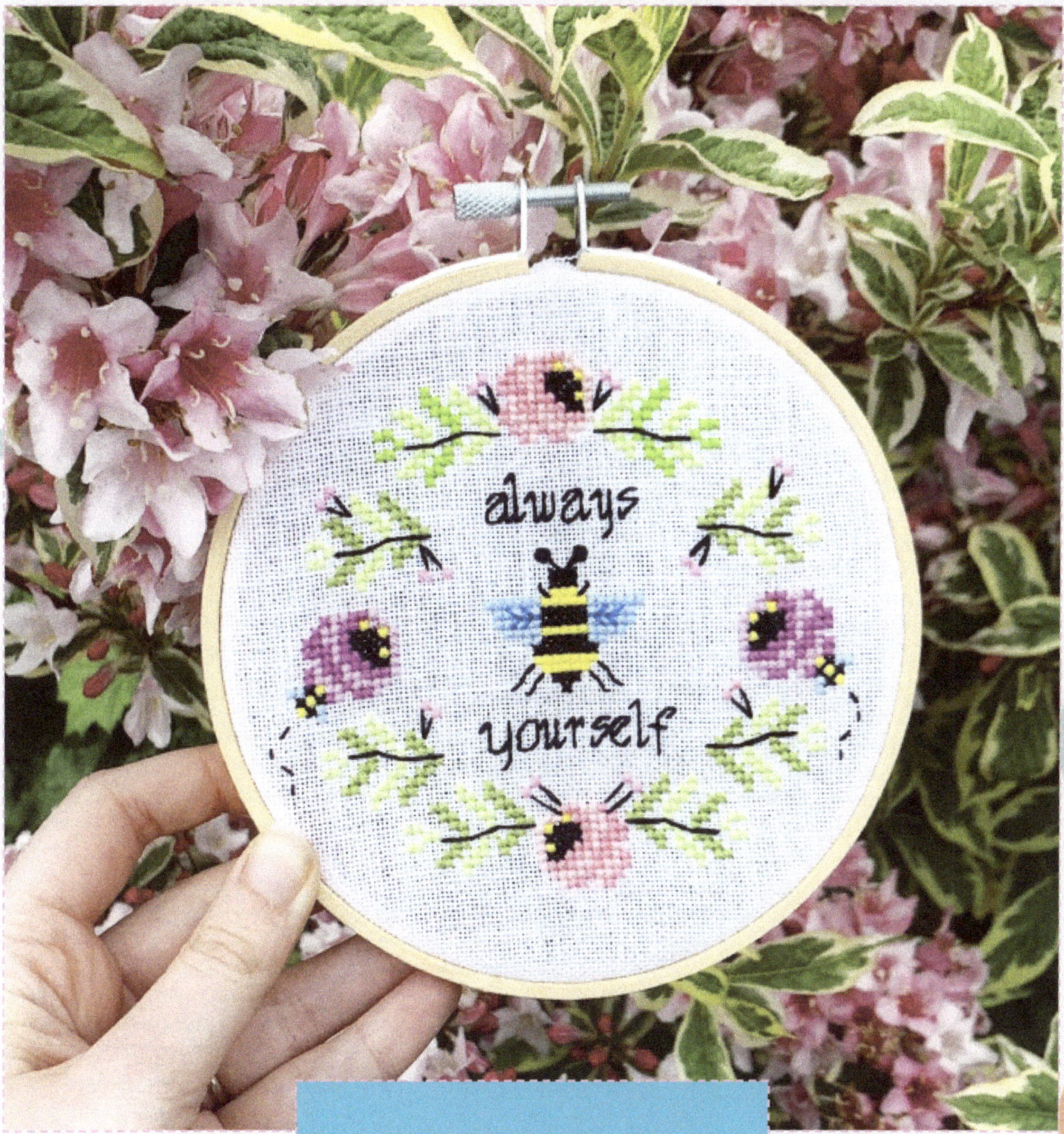

stitch me
in a 5 inch hoop
on 14 count aida
size 20cm x 20cm

	Number	Name:	Strands	Estimated Length	Stitches
✖	DMC 310	Black	3	302.6 cm	86
➕	DMC 156	Blue Violet MD LT	3	8.7 cm	0
⊏	DMC 157	Blue Cornflower V LT	3	93.5 cm	52
−	DMC 963	Ultra V LT Dusty Rose	3	111.5 cm	62
a	DMC 3708	Melon LT	3	129.5 cm	72
C	DMC 307	Lemon	3	77.3 cm	43
Y	DMC 907	Green Parrot LT	3	259.0 cm	144
S	DMC 013	Green Ultra	3	417.2 cm	232
●	DMC 209	Lavender DK	3	107.9 cm	60
▢	DMC 211	Lavender LT	3	129.5 cm	72

BLOOM WHERE YOU ARE PLANTED

BLOOM WHERE YOU ARE PLANTED

stitch me

in a 6 inch hoop

on 14 count aida

size 20cm x 20cm

BLOOM
WHERE YOU ARE
PLANTED

	Number	Name:	Strands	Estimated Length	Stitches
	DMC 310	Black	3	604.4 cm	44
	DMC 893	Carnation LT	3	188.8 cm	105
	DMC 703	Chartreuse	3	803.8 cm	447
	DMC 955	Green Nile LT	3	278.7 cm	155
	DMC 894	Carnation V LT	3	115.1 cm	64
	DMC 554	Violet LT	3	230.2 cm	128
	DMC 307	Lemon	3	336.3 cm	187
	DMC 209	Lavender DK	3	71.9 cm	40
	DMC 963	Ultra V LT Dusty Rose	3	291.3 cm	162
	DMC 975	Brown Golden DK	3	21.6 cm	12
	DMC 747	Blue Sky V LT	3	212.2 cm	118
	DMC 702	Kelly Green	3	57.5 cm	32
	DMC 445	Lemon LT	3	46.8 cm	26

HOME IS WHERE THE PLANTS ARE

HOME IS
WHERE THE
PLANTS ARE

stitch me

in a 6 inch hoop

on 14 count aida

size 20cm x 20cm

	Number	Name:	Strands	Estimated Length	Stitches
	DMC 310	Black	3	563.8 cm	0
Σ	DMC 3348	Yellow Green LT	3	37.8 cm	21
♣	DMC 3347	Yellow Green Med	3	64.7 cm	36
ⅰ	DMC 703	Chartreuse	3	485.5 cm	270
✚	DMC 702	Kelly Green	3	516.1 cm	287
Y	DMC 208	Lavender V DK	3	68.3 cm	38
Ƨ	DMC 3609	Plum Ultra LT	3	124.1 cm	69
W	DMC 307	Lemon	3	156.5 cm	87
◖	DMC 3772	Desert Sand V DK	3	66.5 cm	37
☾	DMC 904	Green Parrot V DK	3	39.6 cm	22
⊘	DMC 157	Blue Cornflower V LT	3	136.7 cm	76
N	DMC 605	Cranberry V LT	3	260.8 cm	145
Ⅱ	DMC 603	Cranberry	3	361.5 cm	201

CELEBRATE THE TINY VICTORIES

CELEBRATE THE TINY VICTORIES

stitch me
in a 6 inch hoop
on 14 count aida
size 20cm x 20cm

	Number	Name:	Strands	Estimated Length	Stitches
◖	DMC 310	Black	3	654.6 cm	364
a	DMC 963	Ultra V LT Dusty Rose	3	223.0 cm	124
◖	DMC 3708	Melon LT	3	223.0 cm	124
▯	DMC 307	Lemon	3	55.7 cm	31
▣	DMC 703	Chartreuse	3	424.4 cm	236
✖	DMC 3772	Desert Sand V DK	3	190.1 cm	38
↗	DMC 3607	Plum LT	3	100.7 cm	56
◗	DMC 208	Lavender V DK	3	208.6 cm	116
▽	DMC 3348	Yellow Green LT	3	521.5 cm	290

THANKS A BUNCH

THANKS A BUNCH FOR BEING YOU

stitch me

in a 6 inch hoop

on 14 count aida

size 20cm x 20cm

	Number	Name:	Strands	Estimated Length	Stitches
✚	DMC 310	Black	3	1383.6 cm	413
▣	DMC 307	Lemon	3	246.4 cm	137
3	DMC 3772	Desert Sand V DK	3	1003.5 cm	558
O	DMC 3855	Autumn Gold LT	3	600.6 cm	334
N	DMC 893	Carnation LT	3	124.1 cm	69
◇	DMC BLANC	White	3	28.8 cm	16
⊞	DMC 894	Carnation V LT	3	174.4 cm	97

FIRST I DRINK THE COFFEE

stitch me

in a 5 inch hoop

on 14 count aida

size 20cm x 20cm

	Number	Name:	Strands	Estimated Length	Stitches
C	DMC 3846	Turquoise Bright LT	3	338.1 cm	188
X	DMC 747	Blue Sky V LT	3	1005.3 cm	559
b	DMC 453	Gray Shell LT	3	118.7 cm	66
☢	DMC 894	Carnation V LT	3	111.5 cm	62
∧	DMC 975	Brown Golden DK	3	244.6 cm	136
O	DMC BLANC	White	3	176.2 cm	98
N	DMC 310	Black	3	334.8 cm	15
⊟	DMC 893	Carnation LT	3	151.1 cm	84

IT'S OK TO
TAKE A BREAK

stitch me
in a 6 inch hoop
on 14 count aida
size 20cm x 20cm

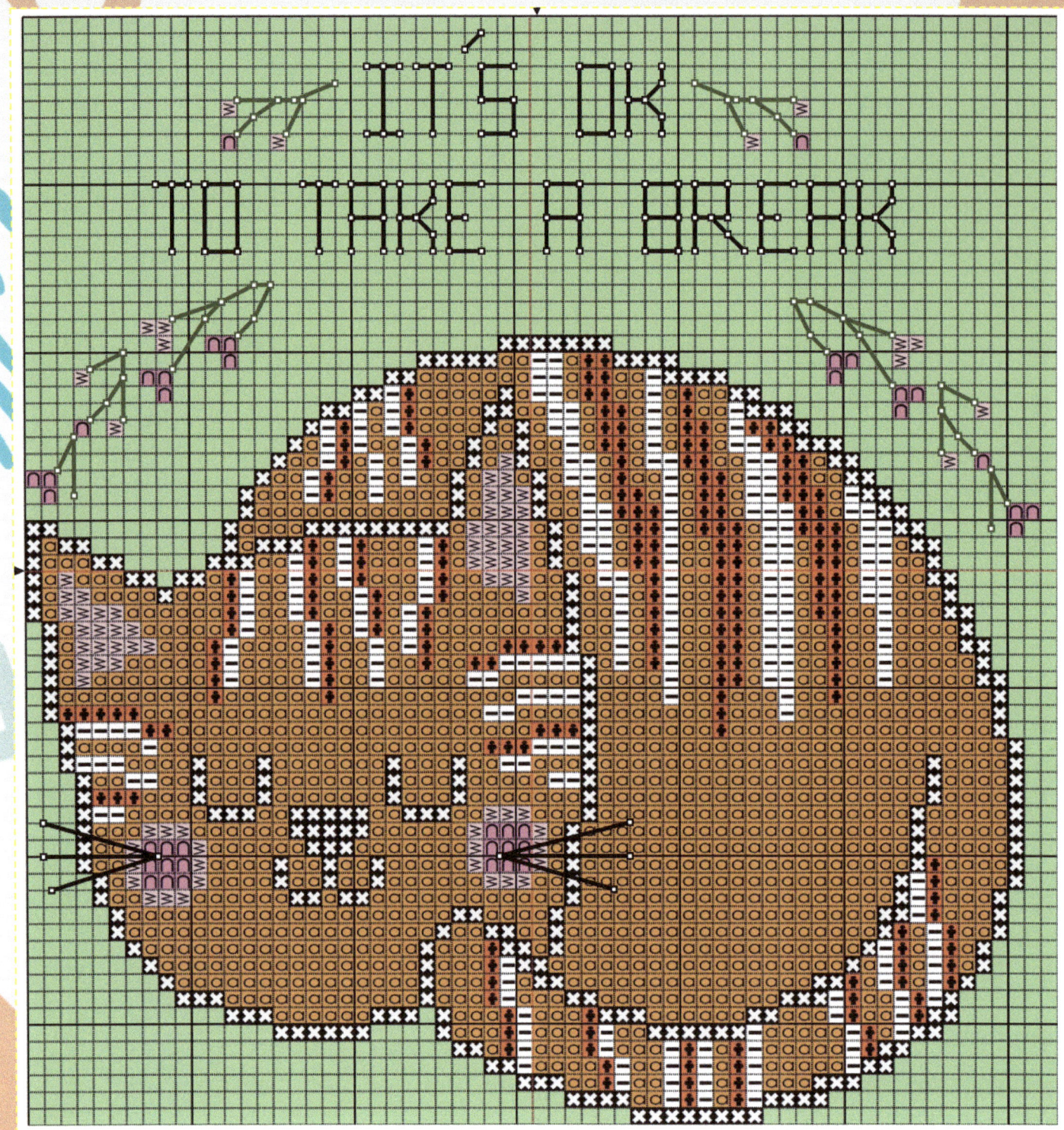

	Number	Name:	Strands	Estimated Length	Stitches
✖	DMC 310	Black	3	677.5 cm	320
✚	DMC 947	Burnt Orange	3	365.1 cm	203
–	DMC BLANC	White	3	408.2 cm	227
a	DMC 741	Tangerine MD	3	2292.9 cm	1275
w	DMC 963	Ultra V LT Dusty Rose	3	149.3 cm	83
n	DMC 604	Cranberry LT	3	71.9 cm	40
o	DMC 904	Green Parrot V DK	3	42.8 cm	0

We firmly believe that stitching is great for improving mental health and people's wellbeing as having a fun little project waiting for you at home really does lift your spirits! Plus, when you are counting stitches you really can't focus on anything else. Over the past two years we have donated thousands of pounds to different causes and charities (with the help of our awesome customers) by creating special cross stitch kits and donating the profits.

We have worked on everything from stitching up cute koalas to help the Aussie animals out who were affected by the wildfires, to stitching up important messages in aid of the charity 'Mind' and more recently a 'Black Lives Matter' rainbow design to help raise funds to support this very important cause and raise awareness.

More recently we have been stitching up rainbows and donated the funds to NHS charities who have been affected the worst by the pandemic.

We believe that stitching is a great way to help support causes whilst also getting some fun projects to stitch up as well!

Here you will find a load of FAQ's about cross-stitching in general, for all info relating to our cross stitch club & products please visit our site www.thegeekystitchingco.com

What is thread count?

You may have noticed all patterns are to be stitched on 14 count aida fabric. The count of thread is the amount of stitches that forms a 1 inch (2.5cm) block. The higher the number, the higher the amount of stitches per inch and therefore the higher the thread count.

How do I calculate the amount of material I need?

In this book we advise the size of material needed for each pattern however it is advisable to add 5cm in each direction to your fabric. If you are unsure of the size of material needed, there is a way to calculate this. Firstly, grab your pattern and count the number of stitches in each direction then divide this by your fabric count (how many stitches per 1 inch) for example, 120 stitches / 14 count (14 stitches per inch) is 8.5 inch or 22cm approximately. You then need to add on your 5cm in each direction.

What is stranded cotton?

The Cotton or Floss that needs to be purchased for cross stitching (We use the brand DMC who are the market leader) comes in a 'Skein' made up of an 8M length of thread which is made up of 6 individual strands. For all our patterns (and most cross stitching designs) 3 of these strands need to be used (otherwise the thread will be too thick) you just need to separate out three stands from a 30cm length of material but always make sure to keep all your thread as this will be used at a later date

How do I find out where the centre of my material is?

The easiest way to find out where the centre of your material is to fold your material in half and then in half again, where all the folds cross is the centre. You can use a water repellent fabric pen to draw a few guidelines direct on to your fabric which you can then wash off at the end of your project in warm water.

What type of Needle do I need to buy?

You need to purchase a blunt tapestry cross stitching needle in size 24 – 28

What type of hoop shall I buy?

We recommend a wooden embroidery hoop with a brass or silver/gold fastening, as you will be able to adjust the tension on your material as you go. There are other items available such as a flexi hoop or Q Snap but these are a little more tricky to use

What happens if I mess up?

Firstly, don't worry! At some point every stitcher will make a mistake and the best thing to do is to carefully unpick all the stitches you have done so you are back to a point where you know its correct. You can buy an un-picker tool or just use your embroidery scissors (just be careful not to cut the actual material!) to carefully cut away the thread. Don't be tempted to 'frog' it, which means carry on and hoping for the best! As at some point the pattern will be incorrect and won't match up correctly.

Can I sell the patterns I create?

The short answer is no. All of our patterns are original and are copyrighted by design making them not available for re-sell. Please feel free to stitch up as many of the patterns and you like to share with your buds!

What's the best way to complete a pattern?

The best way is to always start from the middle and work outwards. We like to work a section at a time (rather than doing all the yellow colour for example) and then move onto another section. We like to work our stitches in one direction first rather than completing each individual stitch as its much quicker

How do I keep my stitching neat?

The best way to keep your stitching neat is to make sure that your stitches are always in the same direction either // or \\ this will give you a great finish. It doesn't matter if you do individual stitches or work a line of stitches at a time, which ever you prefer. It's also a good Idea to not drag your thread over a white empty space on the pattern. Wherever there is a gap in the pattern tie it off at the back and restart again, the back of your pattern should be as neat as the front (apparently!)

How do I do backstitch and how many strands of thread should I use?

Backstitch is demonstrated as a coloured line on the pattern. Firstly, make a single straight stitch, continue along the pattern but come up the space ahead and bring your needle down the same hole of the last stitch you made. We recommend using two strands of thread for any backstitch but if you prefer to use three that is totally fine!

Are Unicorns real?

Duh, of course they are!

CONTACT US

We love to chat all things stitchy! If you have any questions at all about the patterns in this book or just general cross stitching questions please contact us

Email – hello@thegeekystitchingco.com
Website – www.thegeekystitchingco.com
Instagram – geeky_stitching_co
Facebook – The Geeky Stitching Co

Lightning Source UK Ltd.
Milton Keynes UK
UKHW051104200123
415671UK00008B/54